HOW TO PLAY YOUR BEST TENNIS
(For Young Players of all Ages)

Sally Huss

ISBN 13:9780982262542
Huss Publishing
P.O. Box 206, La Jolla, CA 92038
www.sallyhuss.com
www.happychildrensbooks.com

*****

BRIEF REVIEWS

Dick Enberg, CBS and ESPN Sports:

"Loved the book...The message in her book is direct, kind, respectful, and in its wondrous simplicity, as sharp as a backhand winner down the line..."

Billie Jean King, 39 Grand Slam Titles, Founder of World Team Tennis:

"In *Eight Golden Rules for How to Play Your Best Tennis*, Sally Huss shows you how to get the most out of your game and how much fun playing tennis can be."

Mary Carillo, CBS and ESPN Sports:

"Sally Huss has written a simple, sparkling gem of a book. It is wise and gentle...Perhaps her book should be called *Eight Golden Rules for How To Live Your Best Life."*

Eight Golden Rules
for
How to Play Your Best Tennis

Everyone wants to win in tennis. But when you go on the court to play a match, only one player can win, unless of course it's doubles. So how can you tip the scales in your favor? How can you give yourself the best opportunity for winning? By playing your best tennis! And how can you play your best tennis? That's what this book is about.

Tennis is a game of rules and boundaries. There are rules about scoring, etiquette, and the general activities on the court. Then there are the fixed boundaries of the court – the lines. All those who play the game have to abide by these limitations and structures, maneuvering within them. It's the game. But none of these should interfere with your ability to play your best tennis.

There are other rules for that. These are Golden Rules and there are eight of them. These are secret or hidden rules that when followed will allow you to play your best tennis on any given day and on every given day! Learn them. Understand them. Value them. Practice the techniques suggested here and you will play your best tennis every day. Although these are rules, they might also be considered skills, just as valuable as learning how to hit a topspin forehand. Work on them. Develop them, master them, and your best tennis will have the best opportunity of showing up every time you step on the court. Good luck!

Rule #1 – HONOR YOUR BODY

Honor your body for all its worth. It's worth a lot. Without it you could not play tennis or any sport. Keep it in the best shape you can. Nourish it. Hydrate it. Protect it from the sun. After that, be totally appreciative of its efforts whether it's running after a wide forehand or reaching for a lob.

The body with all its miraculous parts is more than willing to do what you ask of it, but it is not always capable. It takes time to learn a new stroke. It takes experience to know where and where not to hit the ball. It takes endurance to play a long match. It takes quickness to volley well and anticipation to get to a drop shot. Be patient. Be appreciative. Be kind.

Your body, like all bodies, has a consciousness all its own. It is aware. Its cells are aware. This consciousness is at about the same level as that of a dog. The kinder you are to it, the more cooperative it is with your desires. Never ever get mad at yourself if you miss a ball, lose a point, or double fault. The body takes this personally and cowers just like a dog would that is being scolded. Besides that, you learn something when you miss a shot. Your body will make adjustments. Be grateful for your body's efforts and patient with its learning.

***Exercise**: At night before you fall asleep take a moment or two to thank your body for its work during the day. Thank your feet and legs for running. Thank your arms for swinging. Thank your hands for gripping, your heart for pumping, your lungs for breathing, your ears and eyes for doing their part. Thank your whole self. Then rest.*

Rule #2 – KEEP A CLEAR MIND

Clear your mind of clutter. When you are learning a new shot or practicing to perfect an old one, your attention is on your own actions. This is normal. But when it's match time, your attention should be on the ball. It should be on the ball in front of you or the one in your hand ready to be served, not on the ball or point you just played.

The mind is a clever instrument that can move back and forward in time and dance all over the place from what you have been taught to what you would like to happen to what you want for dinner. It can concern itself with what a coach or parent may be thinking or wanting to what you should have done on the last shot. Give it a rest. Trust yourself and all that you have learned, including the experience of all the balls you have ever hit. Play the tennis that is in front of you, not the tennis you played yesterday or the tennis you hope to play tomorrow.

One of the most beautiful aspects of tennis is that it involves the whole person -- the physical, emotional and mental levels. But it's the mental one that can trip you up. Keep a clear mind, one without judgment, demands or ramblings and you'll find yourself fully present on the court, ready to pounce when pouncing is required and ready to retrieve when a ball gets away from you. Stay alert!

Exercise: *If you find your mind wandering during a match, blink your eyes a few times to clear your vision. You will be amazed at how quickly your attention pops back to where it should be.*

***Exercise**: Another method for reigning in your attention is to walk the periphery of the court, along the fence line, before you begin a match. Walk all around it, designating it in your mind as your play area, your dance floor, your sports arena. Nothing outside of it has any importance while you are there. Now see how much fun you can have playing and how easy it is to stay focused.*

Rule #3 -- MAINTAIN A POSITIVE ATTITUDE

Attitude is everything. Pick a good one. The best one to pick in order to play your best tennis is a positive one. Your attitude is your point of view, how you see things. Are they scary? Are they worrisome? Or are they wonderful with possibilities of good outcomes? Are they perfect as they are? Does your attitude make you eager or anxious? Get it straight: tennis, like life itself, prefers a happy camper – one who likes where he or she is, but is enthusiastic about participating full out in what's to come. And all with a smile, even if that smile is inside.

To maintain a positive attitude, a smart player lets missed shots and court errors go by the wayside. Such a player relishes winning shots and knows there are more where those came from. Therefore, play fearlessly and eagerly regardless of the score. It's more fun that way too.

<u>Exercise</u>: *Use this mantra now and then on the court or off the court: "I love to play tennis. The more tennis I play, the better I get." Life has a funny way of agreeing with what you say. So say things you like to hear.*

Rule #4 – MAKE THE BALL YOUR BEST FRIEND

Strangely enough the ball always wins in tennis. And the player who is most connected to the ball by controlling it usually wins the match.

Now love is the greatest connector in all things, even tennis. So to love the tennis ball is essential. Make it your best friend. Chase it down when it runs away from you. Send it flying down a sideline when you get the chance. Lob it. Slice it. Drop shot it. Welcome it when it comes toward you from a serve or a returned shot because it allows you the opportunity to send it sailing back across the net. When you love the ball, concentration is easy.

Some players play mad – mad at the court, mad at the umpire, mad at the ball, even mad at themselves. Certainly there is energy in anger. But love trumps anger every time.

When the ball becomes your best friend you are happy to see it coming and just as happy to give it a whack, not because of what it is going to do for you, but for the pleasure of its company. A better time cannot be had than the time spent with friends. Nor can better tennis be played than that which is played in a friendly atmosphere.

<u>Exercise</u>: *Hold a tennis ball in your hand. Feel the fuzzy surface. Squeeze it to feel the tension. Admire the brilliant yellow color. Bounce it a few times with your racket. Realize that it is a magnetic field, like your racket and yourself, and that it is made up of millions of atoms with their electrons and neutrons swirling around. You are connected. Some part of you is connected to the ball, no matter how far across the court you hit it. Feel kindly towards it knowing that your best chance of playing your best tennis is your relationship with the ball. Good friends are hard to find. Be glad you have one on the court, even if it's round and fuzzy.*

Rule #5 – PLAY HAPPY

Play tennis happy – happy inside. Feeling good is the greatest emotional weapon you can have on the court. Happiness is a particular energy that feeds your body, mind and spirit, and puts you in harmony. You cannot play better tennis, than when you, your motions, and emotions are harmonious. Also it is helpful to understand that you cannot play better tennis than you play at any given moment, no matter what you think.

All the tennis you have been taught, all the balls you have hit, all the tennis you've watched on TV, the wind, the sun, the stars in the sky, not to mention your opponent all have a say in how you play at every moment. The earth spins and is never in the same place twice, nor are you. So, it is wise to enjoy the moment and feel yourself in harmony mentally, physically and emotionally as you move around the court.

Anger and disappointment are negative emotions that take you out of harmony. Learn how to increase your energy level with positive emotions. Jump for joy. Pump your fist.

Feel good all the time, whether you win a point or lose it, whether you win a match or lose one. Perfect this skill and no one will ever be able to beat YOU.

Exercise: *In order to feel happy, you have to know where happiness comes from. Take a moment here and say, "I am _________ (state your name)." As you do this, point to yourself. Notice that you have pointed to the center of your chest area. It is a universal phenomenon that when people identify themselves they point to this area. This is the emotional heart center and it is where happiness resides. Touch this spot or think of it and good feeling pours forth. Keep this feeling flowing through you as you play. Play happy!*

Exercise: *Another exercise to help you maintain your happy state while you play is to change the score in your mind to suit your needs. Some players like to be underdogs and come from behind. Others prefer to be ahead and play happier in that position. Try playing as if it were 4-1 in your favor, then play as if it were 1-4 and you are down. What feels better*

to you? Do you thrive on the challenge? Or, do you play better with a safety net of a game or two? Figure out your perfect score, fix it in your mind, and then play with that feeling.

Rule # 6 – FEARLESSLY GO FORWARD

Play free of fear – fear of losing a point or a match. Then you can play your best tennis. Fear tightens your muscles, restricts your actions, and hampers your reactions. It is a useless emotion on the tennis court. Give it up.

The way to play fearlessly is to go on the court prepared to “give" rather than "take." That is, give your attention and effort. If your intention is to “give," you are free. You are not demanding anything back. But if it is to “take” or “get,” whether it’s a point, game, or match, you will be putting pressure on yourself to perform. You will be giving your efforts with ulterior motives. It splits your attention. It moves your focus from what you are doing with the ball to what you want to get back from what you are doing. Hit the ball freely and let it go.

Now it is a bit of a challenge for a player to give up his or her concern for the score or winning, but it is immensely helpful for playing your best tennis. The reason is focus. The ball requires your undivided attention. Keep your focus on the ball and not on the score.

The same is true of any concerns you might have regarding family members, coaches or friends who might be watching your match. What they think is their business. Yours is to play. To play freely is the most fun you can have on a tennis court. Let the results take care of themselves. They always do.

***Exercise**: One of the best ways to experience anything is to do the opposite, then do the thing. To play freely, experiment with a few points or games during a practice match by doing the opposite -- concentrate solely on the score. Tighten all the muscles in your body. Demand of yourself that you win all the points, as if your life depended on it. Think only of the score. See what happens. Then let go and play freely without concern for the score. Play carefree, not careless. Care a lot, but about the ball, not the results. You may be surprised at how much better the results are when you play freely, and how much more fun the game is too.*

***Exercise**: Another method of experiencing the freedom you need to play fearlessly is to enter the court as if you had lost. Try this, when you walk on the court for a match, just pretend that the results are in and you've lost. This takes all the anxiety out of you, but not your opponent. A match appears to be about an outcome -- who will win and who will lose. But in this exercise, the outcome becomes a non-issue. Now you can simply play, and that's when you play your best tennis!*

Rule #7 – FIND THE ZONE

"The zone" is that elusive space in which players feel they play their best tennis. They play as if they were on a different plane. With effortless effort they win points, moving around the court almost ahead of the ball, knowing exactly where the ball is and where to hit it. Players are always looking to get into "the zone." What they don't realize is that they are standing in it, or more precisely it is in them.

Although "the zone" is an internal state, it encompasses everything that is connected to the tennis that is being played -- the players, the balls, the court, the atmosphere, even the audience, if there is one. Perfect focus, harmony, inner joy and active peace are a part of it. It is a state of tremendous uninhibited energy. It is the most desirable state in which to play tennis and in turn it holds the greatest possibility for playing your best tennis.

The conundrum is that the harder a player tries to get into “the zone,” the further away he or she seems to be from it. It is something that happens, not something a player can make happen. A player who can relax the demanding, wanting, desiring portion of the mind and get into the play of the game is more apt to experience “the zone.” When that rational aspect is relaxed, the intuitive aspect can operate. That’s the part that knows everything, takes into account everything, and opens the door for making the best choices. Allow it to operate without asking why or how.

As you know, surprises occur on the court. There are let cords, miss-hits, gusts of wind, bad calls, etc. Be open-minded and delight in the unexpected. When a player has too much going on mentally, he isolates himself from the whole and loses some degree of awareness of what is actually going on, on the court. That player is out of "the zone." The best strategy is to hit the ball where you feel like hitting it at the precise moment you are hitting it. It will be in a better place than any preconceived idea of placement because it will take into account your energy level, your balance, your ability and all of the same for your opponent. Besides this, you will not be sending out any message ahead of time as to where you plan to hit the ball. If you don't know where you're going to hit it until you do, neither will your opponent.

So give yourself every opportunity to play in "the zone" by relaxing physically and mentally, while staying happily focused on the ball.

***Exercise**: Obviously being relaxed is desirable for your movement around the court and your various strokes. But beyond that, there is the opportunity for increased energy with relaxation.*

To prove this, find someone who is willing to try this exercise with you. Stand behind the person and ask him or her to tighten all muscles, as tight as can be. Then reach around the waist of the person and lift him or her off of the ground. Easy.

Now do it again, but ask the person to totally relax all muscles. Notice the difference. If the person is your size or bigger, you probably can't lift the person. A person who is relaxed is infinitely heavier, more powerful, than an uptight person. By tightening, the energy that is flowing everywhere is cut off from the body. By being relaxed a person allows that energy to flow through.

When running around the court, swinging your racket here and there, make sure you have the doors open for that energy to flow. The more energy the better! It's there; use it! And the more you sense that you are a part of the whole event, not the whole event, the more powerful you will become and the more zoneful you will play.

Rule#8 – LET KINDNESS RULE

Kindness is a virtue that can serve you well on and off of the court. If you go on the court with the intention of being kind, your tennis will benefit in many ways. First and foremost the kindness that you send out in various directions goes through you first. You feel it first and that's a good thing. It uplifts you. Then there are all sorts of areas for its use.

Be kind to your opponent. Your opponent is a very important person to your tennis game. Without him or her you would not be able to play. The stronger your opponent is, the more your game is strengthened. The trickier your opponent is, the more versatile your game can become. Value your opponent's abilities and use them to develop yours.

Be generous when it comes to calls and disputes. A little kindness goes a long way to maintaining a harmonious atmosphere.

Whether you are a junior player, senior player, a collegiate competitor, a touring pro or a member of a ladies league team, be kind to umpires, lines people and ball kids, if you have them. They are doing you a favor. Be kind to tennis hostesses, league captains, tournament directors and scheduling people, if they are involved in your game. Many are volunteers. All appreciate a little recognition.

Be especially appreciative of tennis coaches, practice partners and parents who might be assisting you with your tennis.

Be kind to your partner if you are playing doubles. Everyone misses a ball, but no one intends to. And the same goes for yourself -- be kind to yourself, if you miss a ball. A few missed balls only show you where there is room for improvement. A few kind words to yourself during a slump can put a smile back on your face. Kindness is good. Kindness is wise. Kindness is necessary.

Exercise: Realizing that we are all brothers and sisters under the skin, makes it easy to extend kindness to everyone. Take one practice match, whether it's singles or doubles, and play it with exceptional kindness. Give every close call to your opponent or opponents. Give all advantages away. Play hard, but play friendly and see what happens.

Do you play better with this generous attitude or with a greedy one?

CONCLUSION

Tennis is a sport for a lifetime. You can never learn all there is to learn, nor play a perfect, error-free match. But you can gather as many tools for your arsenal as possible – slices, topspins, drop shots, lobs, and a variety of serves. You can learn to stay within the lines and follow the rules, including these Eight Golden Rules.

There are, of course, exceptions to every rule and you can find examples of top players who do not abide by these Eight Golden Rules. But the suggestion here is that you will play your best tennis using them. Use them with the understanding that you have nothing to lose in a match and everything to gain, even if you are the top-seeded player in a tournament. Every player starts a match with the same score. Play to win. It is not important that you win, only that you play to win. Play happily, enthusiastically, freely and full out. Your best tennis is the tennis you play. Remember, everyone wins in tennis because everyone starts with love!

###

To be a champion on the court is one thing. To be a champion of yourself is quite another.

FULL REVIEWS

Dick Enberg, CBS and ESPN Sports:

"Loved the book. I've seen Sally Huss play this great game of tennis. She caressed the ball, while fully embracing the experience. Her style and good form are expressed in her *EIGHT GOLDEN RULES FOR HOW TO PLAY YOUR BEST TENNIS*. It's an extension of her proven championship play. The message in her book is direct, kind, respectful, and in its wondrous simplicity, as sharp as a backhand winner down the line. If I were to start playing again, I'd be best served to read this book FIRST and then GRIP a racquet. Game, Set, and Match, Ms. Huss! Oh My!"

Billie Jean King, 39 Grand Slam Titles, Founder of World Team Tennis: "Tennis is a lifetime sport and fun for players of all ages. In *Eight Golden Rules for How to Play Your Best Tennis*, Sally Huss shows you how to get the most out of your game and how much fun playing tennis can be."

Mary Carillo, CBS and ESPN Sports:

"Sally Huss has written a simple, sparkling gem of a book. It is wise and gentle, and gives to tennis players what the great UCLA coach John Wooden gave to basketball players with his Pyramid of Success. If you do what Sally suggests you will be more than a better player; you'll be a better person. Perhaps her book should be called *Eight Golden Rules for How To Live Your Best Life."*

Peter Smith, Coach USC Men's Tennis Team:

"Sometimes the best advice is the most simple. Sally writes a book of reminders that everyone can relate to and learn from. These are guidelines and rules that I am already using with my team. I think every successful coach uses these. Let *EIGHT GOLDEN RULES* be your tennis coach for a winning strategy!"

Bill Kellogg, President of the Southern California Tennis Association:

"I just had the pleasure of reading Sally Huss' newest addition to tennis literature: *EIGHT GOLDEN RULES* -- For young players of all ages (I love the byline!)

I truly enjoyed it, from start to finish, and there is no question in my mind that she has captured the essence of the game. It takes most people a lifetime to figure out that welcoming challenge and learning to enjoy your time on the court leads to playing your best tennis and loving the sport. Those who read her short book will have the chance to accelerate this learning process and will take away a brand new perspective on how to reach their tennis potential and have fun doing it.

By the way, after reading it, I gave it to my wife just before she headed up north to compete in a dog show. She was very nervous about the prospect of being in the ring and was imagining everything that could go wrong. After reading the book, she adopted a new attitude and won 1st place in her Novice Rally class two days later. Sally's advice applies to life – not just to tennis."

Franklin Johnson, Former President of the United States Tennis Association:

"Loved Sally Huss' tennis book *EIGHT GOLDEN RULES*. It contains such wisdom and terrific advice that is valuable for players at any level. The insights contained in this book are useful to all players and I hope many will be able to access Sally's excellent treatise."

Dodo Cheney, Tennis Hall of Fame Inductee:

"Sally Huss' *EIGHT GOLDEN RULES FOR HOW TO PLAY YOUR BEST TENNIS* is right down my alley. I always tell people, 'It's not how well you play that counts; it's how much you enjoy it that counts.' I have loved competing in tournaments all over the world for over 85 years and have established a record of 386 gold balls (representing national titles.) I really enjoyed this book and if I had read it 50 year ago and applied Sally's Eight Golden Rules earlier I might have 400 gold balls by now!"

ABOUT THE AUTHOR

A former Wimbledon semi-finalist, and National and Wimbledon Junior Champion, Sally (Moore) Huss has played tennis all of her life. She was raised in Bakersfield, California and taught the game by the master teaching pro George Toley at the Los Angeles Tennis Club. Toley was also the long-time head coach of the USC Men's Tennis Team.

Huss gathered championships and rankings during her younger years. Then through her work in dance therapy, Zen and tai chi she created a unique way of playing tennis that she taught privately in Beverly Hills and Malibu. Harcourt, Brace published a book on her method titled HOW TO PLAY POWER TENNIS WITH EASE. Later she and her husband Marv, who was also an excellent player, developed and operated The Aspen Club, a large tennis and sports facility in Colorado, where Sally was the head teaching pro.

With their young son Michael, Marv and Sally returned to California in the late 70's, where Sally put away her rackets to pursue an art and writing career. This resulted in 26 Sally Huss Galleries across the country. Within a few years she picked her rackets up again and started competing in senior events, collecting more titles and gold balls. At the same time she began speaking to tennis, sports and corporate groups on her philosophy regarding the relationship between happiness and success or winning.

Presently, Sally writes and paints in her La Jolla, California studio, creates her King Features syndicated panel *Happy Musings* for newspapers, and happily plays social tennis several times a week as well as participates in women's league matches as a member of the La Jolla Beach and Tennis Club team. Although no longer competing in senior events, Sally is proof of the saying that tennis is, indeed, a sport for a lifetime.

TITLES AND RANKINGS

1955 -- Runner Up National 15 and Under Championship, Ranked #1 in U.S. 15 and Under Division

1958 – Winner U.S. Junior Championship, Winner Wimbledon Junior Championship, Ranked #1 in U.S. 18 and Under Division, Named top Girls' Junior Player of the Decade

1959 – Semi-finalist Wimbledon Championship, Winner U.S. Clay Court Championship, Member of the U.S. Wightman Cup Team, Ranked #4 in the U.S. Women's Division

1980 -- Winner of the National 40 Hard Court Championship, Member of the U.S. Young Cup Team, Ranked #1 in the U.S. Women's 40 Division

1985 – Winner of National 45 Hard Court Championship, Ranked #1 in the 35, 40, 45 Divisions in Southern California, Ranked #1 in the U.S. Women's 45 Division

1986, 1987, 1988 – Ranked #1 in the 45 Division Southern California

2010 – Bronze Ball Winner the U.S. 70's Hard Court Championship with partner Sheila Palmer

2011 -- Gold Ball Winner the U.S. 70's Hard Court Championship with parnter Sheila Palmer

OTHER BOOKS BY SALLY HUSS

A BOAT FULL OF ANIMALS
(Developing 30 Positive Character Traits in Children)
Includes 30 lessons every child should learn --
Huss Publishing

HOW TO GET YOUR MAN
(The Slam-Dunk Formula to Getting the Love of Your Life)
Sally's personal story from Wimbledon to Motherhood --
Huss Publishing

A MILLION REASONS TO BE HAPPY
(A Practical Guide to a Better Now)
Exercises in happiness for parents, teachers, and kids --
Huss Publishing

HOW THE COW JUMPED OVER THE MOON
(The Importance of Trying Something New)
A children's book about making an effort --
Huss Publishing

LITTLE LONELY LEIGH
(The Importance of Believing in Yourelf)
A children's book about self-confidence and friendship --
Huss Publishing

EVERY CHILD COUNTS
(The Importance of Children and Numbers)
A children's book filled with multi-cultural children --
Huss Publishing

A TO Z ANIMAL GAMES

(Games to Develop 26 Positive Habits)
A children's books of fun animal games for every letter --
Huss Publishing

CHUCK AND THE CONSTIPATED CAT
(The Importance of Facing Fears)
A fun children's book about change and daring to try something new --
Huss Publishing

LTTLE BABY BOBBY GOES TO THE ZOO
(The Importance of Understanding 'NO')
A children's books about following directions and valuing children --
Huss Publishing

MR. CONSEQUENCES SAYS 'NO' TO STRANGERS
(Kids' Safety Tips -- first book in a series)
A children's book to help children become aware of the dangers a stranger may pose --
Huss Publishing

THE LITTLE LEPRECHAUN WHO LOVED YELLOW
(The Importance of Following Your Heart)
A children's book about a little leprechaun who followed his heart and got more than what he was looking for --
Huss Publishing

THANKSGIVING DINNER
(A Whimsical Children's Book on Being Thankful)
Huss Publishing

THE TREE-WITHIN-THE TREE
(The Importance of Appreciation)
A childrens' Christmas book about discovering the spirit within all things using the tool of appreciation --
Huss Publishing

ASPEN HUSTLE
(Bobby Riggs and the Opening of The Aspen Club)
A Battle of the Sexes with Sally and Bobby --
Huss Publishing

10 GREAT THOUGHTS ON LOVE
(The Best Love Thoughts Ever)
Huss Publishing

10 GREAT THOUGHTS ON FRIENDSHIP
(Thoughts on Friendship Worth Remembering)
Huss Publishing

LARA TAKES CHARGE
(For very Young Children with Diabetes)
HPLI Books

I LOVE YOU WITH ALL YOUR HEARTS
(The Many Ways a Mother Loves her Child)
Tommy Nelson

www.sallyhuss.com and www.happychildrensbooks.com

4270880R10020

Made in the USA
San Bernardino, CA
08 September 2013